Burn the Ships
A 30-Day Journey to Emotional and Spiritual Healing

by Melinda Haynes

Copyright © 2025 by Melinda Haynes
All rights reserved.
No part of this publication may be reproduced, distributed, or transmitted in any form or by any means—including photocopying, recording, or other electronic or mechanical methods—without prior written permission from the author, except for brief quotations used in reviews, articles, or scholarly works.

Scripture quotations, unless otherwise noted, are taken from the Holy Bible, New International Version. Copyright © 1973, 1978, 1984, 2011 by Biblica, Inc.. Used by permission. All rights reserved worldwide.

This is a work of nonfiction based on the author's personal experience and professional insights. It is intended for inspirational and educational purposes and is not a substitute for professional therapy or medical advice.

Cover art and interior design by Melinda Haynes.

ISBN: 979-8-9990654-0-7

First Edition – 2025

Published by Harbor & Quill Publishing
www.HarborQuill.com
Author: www.MelindaHaynes.com

HARBOR
& QUILL
PUBLISHING

Dedication

First and foremost, to my Lord and Savior Jesus Christ —
the One who gave me the courage to light the match.

To my family —
for your patience, prayers, and unconditional love.

To every trauma survivor who's ever wondered if healing is possible —
I pray these words offer a glimpse that it just might be.

May this book bring hope where there was once only survival,
and may you find, in these pages, the courage to never look back.

To an amazing musical band, For King and Country —
whose song Burn the Ships lit a spark I couldn't ignore.
Thank you for giving language to the moment I knew I couldn't go back.

Table of Contents

DEDICATION I

TABLE OF CONTENTS III

ACKNOWLEDGEMENTS V

A NOTE TO THE READER VI

PREFACE VII

INTRODUCTION IX

DAY 1: BURN THE SHIPS 1

DAY 2: THE LONG DRIVE 3

DAY 3: WHEN GOD SINGS OVER YOU 5

DAY 4: LEAVING WITHOUT CLOSURE 7

DAY 5: SURVIVAL MODE IS NOT A SIN 9

DAY 6: TRADING THE WEIGHT 12

DAY 7: HOPE ON REPEAT 14

DAY 8: BRAVERY IN THE STORM 16

DAY 9: UNCHARTED TERRITORY 19

DAY 10: THE INVISIBLE HAND 22

DAY 11: ONE STEP CLOSER 25

DAY 12: THE POWER OF PAUSE 28

DAY 13: THE POWER OF PERSPECTIVE 31

DAY 14: COURAGE IN THE WAITING 34

DAY 15: FAITH OVER FEELINGS 37

DAY 16: THE GIFT OF GRACE 40

DAY 17: WHEN NUMBING OUT FEELS SAFE 43

DAY 18: A LIFE OF PURPOSE 46

DAY 19: TRUSTING GOD IN TRANSFORMATION 49

DAY 20: GOD'S PROVISION IN THE WILDERNESS 53
DAY 21: LAY DOWN YOUR WEAPONS 56
DAY 22: TRUSTING GOD'S SOVEREIGNTY IN OUR CIRCUMSTANCES 60
DAY 23: JOY IN SUFFERING...63
DAY 24: WAITING PATIENTLY ON GOD'S TIMING..............66
DAY 25: THE POWER OF FORGIVENESS...............................69
DAY 26: GRIEVING WITH HOPE 72
DAY 27: ANGER—HARNESSING THE POWER WITHIN 75
DAY 28: LIVING OUT YOUR FAITH 78
DAY 29: WHEN EFFORTS FALL SHORT—FINDING GRACE IN UNMET EXPECTATIONS 81
DAY 30: THE POWER OF COMMUNITY 85
REFERENCES 88
APPENDIX – REFERENCES BY TOPIC 91
ABOUT THE AUTHOR...94

Acknowledgements

To my clients and readers — your courage to face the hard things continues to inspire me. This book is for you.

To Dr. Kevin Neiman — thank you for being the steady, wise voice in my early career. Your clinical guidance and unwavering support of me as a new grad helped shape not just the therapist I became, but the healer I'm still becoming.

To the early readers, encouragers, and unseen hands who helped me shape these pages — your quiet support made all the difference.

And finally, to the presence behind the scenes — the ones who helped hold the vision when it felt too heavy. Thank you for seeing the heart of this project and helping me bring it into the light.

With love and gratitude,
Melinda

A Note to the Reader

This devotional is designed as a tool for self-reflection, spiritual growth, and personal development. While it provides insights and encouragement, it is not intended to replace professional therapy or counseling. If you are experiencing emotional distress or need mental health support, please seek help from a licensed therapist or mental health professional.

Preface

About four and a half years ago, Katie and I hit the open road. On the surface, it looked like a fun adventure — van life. But the truth underneath was heartbreaking for both of us.

We were leaving a painful situation behind, with just a few personal items in storage and the rest crammed into suitcases in the back of an empty cargo van.

I drove — and prayed — and cried from Chico to somewhere near Modesto.

Then, a song came on the radio. I later learned it had been out for a while, but I had never heard it before. I can't explain it, but it felt like God Himself was singing the words to me. (Yes — God does sing over us. See Zephaniah 3:17.) It felt as though He had placed that song on the band's heart for this exact moment, just for me.

Katie was dozing off in the passenger seat. I put the song on repeat. My tears of sadness slowly turned into tears of gratitude and hope. I was confident God was in the details — and somehow, we were going to be okay.

When we finally pulled into the truck stop in Tehachapi, I found the music video online. There's a scene where the ship explodes, and the characters jump into the sea. That moment is etched into my soul. It was a picture of our life — or rather, our *old* life.

Blown up.

Gone.

And Katie and me swimming to shore.

I eventually learned that the song's personal backstory is different from mine. But in that moment — when I needed something to hold on to — the lyrics fit. They healed something inside me. They reminded me that God's ways are *higher* than ours, and His Word never returns to Him void.

A few months later, we got a custom conversion on the van to turn it into a cute little RV. And we did a lot of exploring and sightseeing. And healing. Lots of healing. And that is how this devotional was born.

So let me ask you:

What has God spoken over you?
What ships do you need to burn today?

Introduction

God created us as whole beings—physical, emotional, and spiritual. But in much of modern church culture, emotional pain is often overlooked, treated as a sign of weak faith, or over-emphasized as the ultimate "experience" with God. None of these align with the gospel.

From Genesis to Revelation, God meets His people in their deepest places of sorrow, fear, joy, shame, and hope. The Bible contains over 3,000 verses that directly express human emotion—and God is never intimidated by our feelings. He meets us in them.

This devotional is for those walking through trauma, transition, or transformation. It's for the ones who need to leave a painful past in the past. For the ones who feel weary, stuck, or unsure how to move forward. It's for anyone ready to heal—not just spiritually, but emotionally too.

The title *Burn the Ships* comes from the historic legend of Hernán Cortés, a Spanish conquistador who reportedly ordered his men to burn their ships to eliminate the option of going back. They had no choice but to press forward. All in. No turning back. While history complicates the original story, the metaphor endures: there comes a time to stop rehashing your past and start claiming your future.

In this context, "burning the ships" means letting go of what once helped you survive—shame, fear, control, addiction, people-pleasing, regret—and choosing to move forward into wholeness.

God says: *"Forget the former things; do not dwell on the past. See, I am doing a new thing!"* (Isaiah 43:18–19).

This 30-day devotional combines Scripture, trauma-informed insight, and practical action steps to help you move forward—not perfectly, but honestly.

Welcome to *Burn the Ships*—a soul-searching devotional for when there's just no going back.

Day 1: Burn the Ships

Scripture: "If anyone is in Christ, the new creation has come: The old has gone, the new is here!" — 2 Corinthians 5:17

Devotional Reflection

It didn't feel brave at the time. It felt like panic. Like survival. Like desperation. Katie and I threw a few belongings into a van and drove away from everything familiar — not because we had a grand plan, but because we knew we couldn't stay.

Our old life had burned down. Emotionally. Spiritually. Relationally. And yet, in the middle of the wreckage, I knew: We were never going back.

And like the Spanish conquistador who ordered his men to burn their ships I knew there could be no retreat. No turning back. Fully committed to our "New World," whatever that would be.

I didn't know where we were going. But I knew what God had made clear: that previous chapter was over.

Therapeutic Insight

From a psychological standpoint, trauma can bind us to the past in ways that make moving forward feel difficult. When you've experienced trauma, loss, or deep emotional upheaval, your brain often clings to the familiar— even if the familiar was unhealthy. It's part of a psychological concept called "trauma bonding" — where you may feel drawn back to the very place or people that hurt you (Carnes,1997).

Burning the ships isn't about reckless abandonment — it's about intentional *disconnection from what no longer serves your healing.*

It's choosing to tell your nervous system: *I am safe now. I don't need to go back there to survive.*

Reflection Questions

What are the "ships" in your life that represent the past you've been called out of?

Are there relationships, beliefs, or patterns you've been tempted to return to out of comfort — even though they're no longer good for you?

Actionable Step

Write down one relationship, habit, or belief that you need to leave behind—and then physically destroy the paper (safely), symbolizing your commitment to let go.

Prayer

God, help me let go of what You've called me out of. Give me the strength to not just leave my old life behind — but to release my grip on it completely. Burn the "ships" that lead back to shame, fear, and dysfunction. Help me believe that what You have ahead is greater than what's behind. Amen.

Day 2: The Long Drive

Scripture: "The Lord is near to the brokenhearted and saves the crushed in spirit." — Psalm 34:18

Devotional Reflection

I remember the road. Not the scenery — just the silence, the darkness, the ache, the tears I tried to hide from Katie while she slept.

We'd left Chico hours earlier. Every mile felt both freeing and terrifying. I kept wondering if we'd made the right decision. I was exhausted, physically and emotionally, but the road gave me no choice but to keep moving forward.

And then — the song.

One I'd never heard before- even though I'd find out later that it had been a radio favorite for a while. But it felt like God had personally kept it hidden for me, right in this moment. Not a random track on a station's playlist, but a message from heaven saying, *"I see you. I've got you."*

Burn the Ships by For King and Country.

I played it on repeat.

And somewhere between Modesto and Tehachapi, the tears stopped being about pain — and started being about hope.

Therapeutic Insight

When you leave a high-stress, toxic, or traumatic environment, your nervous system can remain in "survival mode" long after the danger has passed. This is called hypervigilance — a common trauma response where your brain stays alert, scanning for threats.

This is normal. You're not broken.

But healing begins when you recognize what safety feels like — even in small moments. A song, a deep breath, the presence of someone kind. These are *glimmers* — the opposite of triggers — and they help retrain your brain to trust again (Dana, 2021).

Glimmers are God's grace in motion.

Reflection Questions

What was a "glimmer" moment for you — a time you sensed peace even in the middle of fear?

What does your body need to feel safe right now?

How might God be showing up in subtle ways that you've overlooked?

Actionable Step

Create a "glimmer list"—a written collection of small moments that bring you comfort or peace. Add to it daily to retrain your brain to seek out beauty and safety.

Prayer

God, thank You for meeting me on the road — not just the one beneath my wheels, but the one in my heart. I confess I still carry fear, even as I try to move forward. Help me notice the glimmers of Your presence. Calm my racing thoughts. Remind me that I don't walk alone. Amen.

Day 3: When God Sings Over You

Scripture: "The Lord your God is with you, the Mighty Warrior who saves. He will take great delight in you; in his love he will no longer rebuke you, but will rejoice over you with singing." — Zephaniah 3:17

Devotional Reflection

I'd heard that verse before — the one about God singing over us —and that night on the road, I felt a joyful, personal connection to it. Katie had fallen asleep. I was driving, numb and tired, with nothing but my thoughts and the hum of the highway.

Every lyric wrapped around me like a blanket. Not condemning. Not fixing. Just holding. Singing. Speaking straight to my soul:
"You're not alone."
"You're going to be okay."
"I've got you."

I still didn't know where we were going. But I was starting to believe we weren't lost.

Therapeutic Insight

Music is a powerful tool for emotional regulation. It bypasses logic and speaks directly to the limbic system — the part of the brain that stores memory and processes emotion. When a song resonates deeply, especially in times of distress, it can create a sense of safety and validation, helping to soothe the nervous system and foster healing (Levitin, 2006).

What we experience isn't just comfort — it is *neurobiological repair*. God designed our brains to respond to beauty, rhythm, and connection. When He sings over you — through Scripture, a song, or silence — your soul listens, even if your mind is too tired to understand.

Reflection Questions

Has there ever been a moment when a song felt like it was speaking *directly* to your situation?

How might God be using creativity — music, art, nature, words — to reach you now?

Are you making space to listen?

Actionable Step

Create a 3 song (or longer) playlist that helps you express your emotions or that speaks life to your current season.

Prayer

God, I still don't always know how to hear You. But I want to. Teach me to listen — not just with my ears, but with my spirit. Thank You for singing over me when I have no words of my own. Let Your love be louder than my fear. Amen.

Day 4: Leaving Without Closure

Scripture: "But one thing I do: Forgetting what is behind and straining toward what is ahead, I press on toward the goal to win the prize for which God has called me heavenward in Christ Jesus." — Philippians 3:13-14

Devotional Reflection

Leaving without closure is one of the hardest parts of moving on. The final conversation. The last look. The moment when everything is left unsaid, unfinished. We left behind so many questions, so much confusion, and so many broken pieces of a life that we couldn't make sense of. The ending didn't feel like an ending at all. It felt like an unfinished story.

But as I kept driving, I realized something: the *lack* of closure doesn't mean God's work in our lives was incomplete. Sometimes, He asks us to move forward with *open-endedness*. With questions that may never be answered, wounds that may never fully heal, relationships that may never be restored. He calls us to press on even when we don't have all the answers.

Therapeutic Insight

Leaving without closure is a psychological and emotional challenge — especially when trauma or loss is involved. The brain craves resolution, but often life doesn't offer it. When we don't get the "final chapter" we expect, our minds can feel stuck, ruminating over what was left unresolved.

Therapeutic strategies for managing *unfinished business* include emotional acceptance and self-compassion (Neimeyer, 2001). Acknowledge that the past will likely never feel "complete."

However, by allowing space for grief, surrendering control, and looking to the future, you free yourself to heal. God doesn't need closure to redeem our stories. He makes beauty from brokenness.

Reflection Questions

Is there an area of your life where you've been stuck, hoping for closure or resolution?

What might it look like to give yourself permission to move forward without all the answers?

How can you release control over what you can't change?

Actionable Step

Write a "letter of release" to someone or something you never got closure with. You don't need to send it—just allow your broken pieces to speak freely.

Prayer

God, I don't always understand why things are left unresolved. It's hard to move forward when I feel like I've been left hanging. Teach me to trust You with the things I can't change, the things that hurt, and the parts of my story that are still unfinished. I release my need for closure and place my faith in You. Amen.

Day 5: Survival Mode Is Not a Sin

Scripture: "He gives strength to the weary and increases the power of the weak." — Isaiah 40:29

"But he said to me, 'My grace is sufficient for you, for my power is made perfect in weakness.' Therefore I will boast all the more gladly of my weaknesses, so that the power of Christ may rest upon me." — 2 Corinthians 12:9

Devotional Reflection

In the early days of our journey, I didn't feel brave or strong. I felt like I was just barely holding on. I wasn't thinking about the future. I was surviving the moment. Every mile we drove, every city we passed through, felt like I was just trying to keep my head above water.

And that's okay. Because there are seasons when we don't have the luxury of thriving. We just have to survive.

Sometimes, survival is the most honest thing we can do. When life is too heavy, when hope is distant, the act of simply getting through the day is a victory.

God doesn't require us to be strong all the time. He offers His strength to the weary, His peace to the restless. He meets us in the moments when all we can do is put one foot in front of the other, trusting that He's carrying us even when we don't have the strength to walk.

Therapeutic Insight

Survival mode isn't just a metaphor — it's a real, physiological state. When we experience intense stress, trauma, or loss, the body can go into "fight or flight," where the primary goal is to protect the self, even if that means putting our emotions on autopilot.

In these moments, it's normal to feel disconnected, numb, or just too tired to care about anything beyond getting through.

Survival mode is not weakness. It's your body's response to overwhelming circumstances. And while it can be exhausting, it's also a sign that your body is trying to protect you (van der Kolk, 2014). Healing happens when we acknowledge that survival is valid, and when we allow ourselves grace in those moments of struggle.

Reflection Questions

Have you been too hard on yourself for "just surviving" in difficult seasons?

How can you show compassion toward yourself when you're in survival mode?

What steps can you take today to invite God's strength into your weakness?

Actionable Step

Make a "bare minimum" list for the day—3 small, manageable tasks you can do. Self-care tasks like taking a hot shower or eating a healthy meal count. Allow yourself to rest without guilt after completing them.

Prayer

God, thank You for meeting me in the midst of my exhaustion. I confess that I've often judged myself for just getting through, for not "thriving" at all times. But I know that in my weakness, You are strong. Give me Your strength when I'm weary and remind me that I'm never alone. Amen.

Day 6: Trading the Weight

Scripture: "He heals the brokenhearted and binds up their wounds." — Psalm 147:3

Devotional Reflection

I never wanted to admit the depth of the wounds I carried. The shame. The disappointment. The fear. It was easier to push it all down, to pretend like I was fine, and to keep moving forward. But the reality was that I couldn't move forward without first facing what had been broken inside me.

God knows this about us — He knows that healing begins when we name what hurts. It's not about pointing fingers or assigning blame. It's about acknowledging the wounds so He can bind them up with His love and grace.

The wounds don't define us, but refusing to acknowledge them can keep us stuck. And healing doesn't come in silence. It comes when we bring our pain into the light and let God work in the open spaces.

Therapeutic Insight

In therapy, there's something called naming the wound — identifying the source of pain so it can be treated. This process helps us make sense of what's happened and allows us to begin separating our identity from our pain (Brown, 2012). Until we name our wounds, we often stay stuck in the story of the hurt. Naming them allows us to reclaim control over our narrative.

When we bring our wounds before God, we allow Him to meet us in those broken places and start the process of healing. Healing requires vulnerability, but it also brings restoration. You don't have to stay trapped in the hurt. God can bind up every wound, if you'll let Him.

Reflection Questions

What are the wounds you've been avoiding naming — the ones you've tucked away in your heart?

How might naming your pain in the presence of God help bring healing?

Is there a specific wound you need to surrender today?

Actionable Step

Find a small stone to represent a burden. Hold it in your hand and name exactly what it represents. Then place the stone at the foot of a cross, a tree, or in another symbolic place, proclaiming: *"God, I'm not carrying this anymore."*

Prayer

God, I don't want to keep hiding my wounds from You. They are real, and they hurt, but I trust that You can heal them. I give You permission to touch those deep places in my heart, the ones I've been too afraid to name. Heal me, God, and make me whole again. Amen.

Day 7: Hope on Repeat

Scripture: "For I know the plans I have for you," declares the Lord, "plans to prosper you and not to harm you, plans to give you a hope and a future." — Jeremiah 29:11

Devotional Reflection

I have found that hope isn't always something we *feel* instantly. Sometimes, it's something we have to choose. And sometimes, it's something we have to *remind ourselves* of, again and again.

Just like the song played on repeat, hope needs to be revisited — often. Hope is like a muscle that needs to be exercised regularly to grow strong. Even in the darkest moments, we have the power to choose to believe in God's promises, over and over, until our faith is unshakable.

Therapeutic Insight

Hope is a critical part of emotional resilience. When we go through hardship, it's easy for hope to feel distant or even impossible. But research shows that hope isn't just a passive feeling; it's an active process that involves setting goals, finding pathways, and maintaining the belief that we can achieve those goals.

Practicing hope — by repeating Scriptures, writing down goals, or recalling past victories and blessings— helps us build a "hope muscle" that strengthens our ability to navigate future struggles (Snyder, 2002).

When we practice hope, we're not denying our pain. Instead, we're choosing to partner with God in the ongoing work of restoration.

Reflection Questions

When was the last time you actively chose hope — even when you didn't feel like it?

What's a promise from God you can repeat to yourself in the coming days?

How can you create space in your life to nurture hope, even in small moments?

Actionable Step

Choose a hope-filled affirmation based on Scripture and repeat it aloud to yourself three times each morning.

Example: *being confident of this, that he who began a good work in you will carry it on to completion until the day of Christ Jesus-* Phil. 1:6

"God is not finished with me yet!"

Prayer

God, I know You have plans for my life — plans for good, not harm. When hope feels far away, help me choose to believe in Your promises. Let me repeat Your truth over and over until it takes root in my heart. Strengthen my hope and help me trust You every step of the way. Amen.

Day 8: Bravery in the Storm

Scripture: "For God gave us a spirit not of fear but of power and love and self-control." — 2 Timothy 1:7

"He got up, rebuked the wind and said to the waves, 'Quiet! Be still!' Then the wind died down and it was completely calm." — Mark 4:39

"The Lord will fight for you; you need only to be still." — Exodus 14:14

Devotional Reflection

When we left everything behind, it felt like setting sail into a vast, unknown sea. The winds of fear whipped around us, the waves of uncertainty crashed over us, and yet, we had no choice but to keep moving forward. At times, it felt like being in the middle of a storm — the kind where you wonder if you'll ever see the shore again.

And while I didn't feel brave, I kept hearing this quiet whisper: Bravery isn't about calm waters. It's about sailing through the storm, trusting that the One who called you to the sea will bring you through it.

Sometimes, God does calm the seas, just like He did in Mark 4:39 when Jesus said, "Quiet! Be still!" and the storm instantly stopped.

But other times, He calms His child — like He did in Exodus 14:14, telling His people, "The Lord will fight for you; you need only to be still."

The same God who controls the storm also controls our hearts, and sometimes His greatest work in us is not to change our circumstances, but to change us in the midst of them.

Therapeutic Insight

Fear is a natural response when we're faced with uncertainty, and it often arises when we're stepping into new territory. But bravery on the sea comes from embracing uncertainty and choosing to move forward despite the fear.

In therapy, we often talk about confronting fears as a way of building resilience — the more we face discomfort, the more our capacity to endure and grow is strengthened (Siegel, 2010).

Bravery doesn't mean the absence of fear; it means we act even when fear is present. And when we do, we begin to build confidence that God will either calm the storm around us or calm the storm within us. We can trust that He's with us every step of the way, no matter how the sea behaves.

Reflection Questions

What is the "storm" in your life that has caused fear to rise up in you?

How can you choose to step out in bravery, even if you don't feel ready?

In what ways might God be asking you to trust Him — to calm your heart — even if He doesn't immediately calm your circumstances?

Melinda Haynes

Actionable Step

Identify one small step of faith you've been avoiding due to fear. Can you take that step today, even if it feels uncomfortable?

Prayer

God, I know You're calling me to sail through these stormy waters, not because I am fearless, but because You are with me. Thank You for Your power to calm both the storms around me and the storms within me. Help me trust You as my Captain, guiding me through fear and uncertainty. Give me the bravery to keep going, even when the waves are high. I choose to trust You today, knowing You are bigger than the storms around me. Amen.

Day 9: Uncharted Territory

Scripture: "Your word is a lamp to my feet and a light to my path." — Psalm 119:105

"Trust in the Lord with all your heart and lean not on your own understanding; in all your ways submit to him, and he will make your paths straight."— Proverbs 3:5-6

"I will instruct you and teach you in the way you should go; I will counsel you with my loving eye on you."— Psalm 32:8

Devotional Reflection

The road ahead felt like uncharted territory. Every direction seemed unfamiliar, every turn uncertain. I kept wondering, Is this the right path? The fear of the unknown was overwhelming. But I knew something: the God who led us out of the past would also guide us forward. We didn't need to see the whole map — just the next step.

Stepping into uncharted territory requires trust. It's easy to want clear, defined answers, but often, God asks us to trust Him *one step at a time*. It's like walking through the fog — you may not see the way ahead, but you can trust that His light will reveal just enough to keep going.

God promises to guide us, to instruct us, and to counsel us — even in the darkest places. The key is surrendering the need for certainty, and trusting that He knows the way.

Melinda Haynes

Therapeutic Insight

Venturing into the unknown can trigger anxiety, as we often crave certainty and control. But uncertainty is a natural part of life. In therapy, we talk about tolerating uncertainty as an important skill for emotional health (Hayes, Strosahl, & Wilson, 2016).

When we learn to live in the tension of the unknown, we build resilience and trust in God's leading. Practicing mindfulness in moments of uncertainty — focusing on the present moment and taking one step at a time — can help reduce anxiety and ground us in the knowledge that we don't need to have it all figured out. God's light is enough for today.

Reflection Questions

In what areas of your life do you feel like you're walking in uncertainty?

How can you release the need for control and trust God's guidance, even when the path is unclear?

What is one step of faith you can take today, trusting that God will light the way?

Actionable Step

Practice 5 minutes of mindful stillness. Sit quietly and breathe deeply, feel the presence of God. Lean into trust in Him. Ask Him to light only the next step—not the whole map.

Prayer

Lord, thank You for being my guide in this unfamiliar journey. I don't always know where I'm going, but I trust that You do. Help me surrender the need for certainty and embrace the peace that comes with walking by faith. I trust that You will light my way, one step at a time. Amen.

Day 10: The Invisible Hand

Scripture: "The angel of the Lord encamps around those who fear him, and he delivers them." — Psalm 34:7

"For He will command His angels concerning you to guard you in all your ways." — Psalm 91:11

"Though I walk through the valley of the shadow of death, I will fear no evil, for You are with me; Your rod and Your staff, they comfort me." — Psalm 23:4

Devotional Reflection

There were days, in the midst of it all, when I felt completely alone. The road stretched on, the weight of the journey heavy on my heart, and there wasn't another soul in sight.

But deep down, I knew — we were never really alone. God's presence is a comfort we often take for granted. We may not see Him with our eyes, but He's always there, walking with us, fighting for us, even in the silence. Psalm 34:7 reminds us that the Lord's angels are encamped around those who fear Him, offering protection and deliverance, even when we can't perceive them.

It's easy to feel isolated when we're in the middle of hard times. But God is there, even in the unseen. And sometimes, His greatest work is happening in the invisible — in the things we can't always feel or see.

His angels are surrounding us, His presence is near, and His love is constant, even when the path feels lonely.

Therapeutic Insight

Sometimes, in our hardest moments, we feel as if no one understands or is present. But even when it feels like we're on our own, we are never truly alone. Emotional support is vital in times of stress, and while we might not always see it, it is there. The Bible tells us that God has assigned angels to protect and guide us.

In therapy, we talk about social support as an essential part of healing (Bowlby, 1988). Whether through people, prayer, or even unseen spiritual support, knowing that we're cared for — even if we can't physically see it — can create a sense of peace. Just like God's spiritual support is invisible but real, so too are the networks of care He places around us.

Reflection Questions

When was the last time you felt completely alone, and how did you experience God's presence in that moment?

How can you remind yourself that God's unseen support is always with you, even when you don't feel it?

How can you practice noticing the invisible things God is doing around you today?

Actionable Step

Ask one *trusted* person for prayer or support today, even if it feels vulnerable. Let someone "see" you where you are.

Melinda Haynes

Prayer

Lord, thank You for Your constant presence, even when I can't see or feel You. I trust that You are surrounding me with unseen support — angels, Your Spirit, and the love of those You place in my life. Help me to remember that I'm never alone, no matter how far the road seems. Comfort me today and help me feel the peace of Your presence. Amen.

Day 11: One Step Closer

Scripture: "The Lord makes firm the steps of the one who delights in him." — Psalm 37:23

"I press on toward the goal to win the prize for which God has called me heavenward in Christ Jesus." — Philippians 3:14

"For we walk by faith, not by sight." — 2 Corinthians 5:7

Devotional Reflection

It's easy to feel like we're not getting anywhere when we're in the middle of a journey, especially when the road seems long and the destination distant.

There were times when I wondered if we were really making progress. The steps felt small, the pace slow, and the challenges overwhelming. But God steadied my heart: One step closer.

Progress in the kingdom of God is not always measured by leaps and bounds; often, it's found in the steady, faithful steps we take each day. Psalm 37:23 assures us that the Lord orders our steps — every single one of them.

It's not about how quickly we get there, but about our faithfulness in taking those steps with Him. Sometimes, we just need to remember that each step, no matter how small, is bringing us closer to the goal.

And as we press forward, trusting God's timing, we're becoming more and more like Him — growing in faith, perseverance, and courage. The journey might be long, but it's shaping us every step of the way.

Therapeutic Insight

In therapy, we often talk about small wins and how they are essential for building momentum (Amabile & Kramer, 2011). Whether it's taking a deep breath in a moment of stress or making one positive decision in the face of uncertainty, small steps create real progress.

Even if you can't see the destination, each small victory matters. It's the consistency that leads to change, and when we focus on taking one small step at a time, it reduces the overwhelming feeling of having to "get it all done" at once. God doesn't require perfection — He requires progress.

Reflection Questions

What small step can you take today to move closer to the life God is calling you to?

In what areas have you seen progress, even if it feels small or slow?

How can you encourage yourself to keep pressing on, one step at a time?

Actionable Step

Choose one small goal aligned with your healing journey and complete it today—no matter how minor. Celebrate it as progress.

Prayer

God, thank You for being with me in every step of this journey. When I feel like I'm not getting anywhere, remind me that You are ordering my steps, and every one of them matters. Help me take one faithful step today, trusting that You are guiding me closer to Your perfect plan. Strengthen me to keep pressing on, not in my own strength but in Your grace. Amen.

Day 12: The Power of Pause

Scripture: "Be still, and know that I am God." — Psalm 46:10

"The Lord will fight for you; you need only to be still." — Exodus 14:14

"Come to me, all you who are weary and burdened, and I will give you rest." — Matthew 11:28

Devotional Reflection

Sometimes, the most powerful thing we can do in the middle of a journey is stop. It sounds counterintuitive, doesn't it? We're used to pushing forward, making progress, always moving. But there are moments when God calls us to pause — to be still, to breathe, and to rest in His presence.

When we first hit the road, I had this overwhelming sense that I needed to be doing something. After all, life wasn't going to change if I just sat still.

But God began to teach me that rest isn't laziness. It's trust. Psalm 46:10 says, "Be still, and know that I am God." In the original Hebrew, the word rāphâ means "to let go," "to relax," "to cease striving," "to stop fighting," "to drop your hands."

It's not passive stillness, but active surrender. Being still isn't about disengaging from life — it's about engaging with God. It's in those moments of stillness that He often renews our strength and restores our souls.

Therapeutic Insight

In therapy, we talk about the importance of pausing to allow ourselves to process emotions, thoughts, and even physical sensations.

Often, when life gets overwhelming, we push forward out of a sense of urgency, fear, or anxiety. But taking a moment to pause — whether through deep breathing, mindfulness, or meditation (on God's Word) — can help reduce stress and recalibrate our focus (Kabat-Zinn, 1990).

In doing so, we make space for clarity and peace, and we're reminded that we don't have to do everything in our own strength. God is with us, and sometimes the most powerful thing we can do is simply rest in Him.

Reflection Questions

When was the last time you truly paused and allowed yourself to be still in God's presence?

How can you create space for rest today, even if it's just for a few moments?

What is God inviting you to let go of in order to rest in Him?

Actionable Step

Set a timer for five minutes. Do absolutely nothing but breathe deeply and say this prayer: "You are God and I am not."

Melinda Haynes

Prayer

Lord, thank You for the gift of rest. I confess that sometimes I feel like I need to keep moving, but I trust that You are in the stillness, too. Help me to pause today — to breathe deeply, to listen for Your voice, and to know that You are God. I choose to rest in You, trusting that You are fighting for me and renewing my strength. Amen.

Day 13: The Power of Perspective

Scripture: "Set your minds on things above, not on earthly things." — Colossians 3:2

"For our light and momentary troubles are achieving for us an eternal glory that far outweighs them all. So we fix our eyes not on what is seen, but on what is unseen, since what is seen is temporary, but what is unseen is eternal." — 2 Corinthians 4:17-18

"I have told you these things, so that in me you may have peace. In this world you will have trouble. But take heart! I have overcome the world." — John 16:33

Devotional Reflection

There were times during our journey when I couldn't see beyond the immediate struggles. The weight of everything seemed to eclipse any sense of hope or purpose. Every setback felt like the end of the road. But slowly, God began to shift my perspective. It's so easy to focus on the challenges in front of us — the obstacles, the disappointments, and the fears.

But when we set our eyes only on the things that are right in front of us, we forget the bigger picture. The truth is, God is doing something greater than we can see right now. Colossians 3:2 tells us to set our minds on heavenly things, not on earthly things.

It's a reminder to look beyond the immediate, temporary circumstances and focus on the eternal. The things we see are temporary; the work God is doing in us and through us is eternal. When we shift our focus, we begin to see the world from God's perspective. Suddenly, the things that once seemed overwhelming are seen through the lens of His purpose, His love, and His power.

Therapeutic Insight

One of the core principles in therapy is the power of reframing. When we look at a situation from a different angle, it often changes how we feel about it (Beck, 1979).

By adjusting our perspective, we can shift from seeing challenges as obstacles to seeing them as opportunities for growth. This doesn't mean ignoring the pain or difficulty but acknowledging that how we choose to view the situation plays a huge role in our emotional response.

Practicing cognitive reframing — choosing to focus on the bigger picture and eternal truths — can reduce stress and increase resilience.

When we align our thoughts with God's truth, we experience peace and hope, even in the midst of difficulty. God calls us to focus on what is unseen — the eternal purposes He is working in us.

Reflection Questions

How have your circumstances been affecting your perspective?

How can you shift your focus from temporary struggles to eternal truths today?

What is one truth about God that you can choose to focus on instead of your immediate worries?

Actionable Step

Create a "waiting prayer jar." Write down what you're waiting on God for, fold it, and place it in the jar. Let this be a symbol of trust and surrender of things earthside, as you focus on eternity.

Prayer

Lord, thank You for reminding me that You are working in ways I cannot always see. Help me to shift my perspective and fix my eyes on You — on the eternal glory You are preparing, rather than the temporary struggles I face. I choose to focus on Your promises and trust that You are greater than any challenge I may encounter. Give me peace today as I set my mind on things above. Amen.

Day 14: Courage in the Waiting

Scripture: "Wait for the Lord; be strong and take heart and wait for the Lord." — Psalm 27:14

"But those who hope in the Lord will renew their strength. They will soar on wings like eagles; they will run and not grow weary, they will walk and not be faint." — Isaiah 40:31

"I wait for the Lord, my whole being waits, and in his word I put my hope." — Psalm 130:5

Devotional Reflection

When you're in the middle of a journey, you want to keep moving forward, to see progress, and to feel like you're getting somewhere. But sometimes, the hardest part of the journey is the waiting.

I remember moments when I felt like I had been waiting forever, and I just wanted to be somewhere — anywhere — other than where I was. But God teaches us that waiting isn't passive; it's active. Psalm 27:14 tells us to "wait for the Lord; be strong and take heart."

Waiting is not about standing still and doing nothing. It's about strengthening our hearts and trusting in God's perfect timing. It's in the waiting that He renews our strength, as Isaiah 40:31 reminds us, "those who hope in the Lord will renew their strength."

In the waiting, God is working. He's developing perseverance, refining our faith, and preparing us for what's next. Waiting takes courage because it requires trust. It's acknowledging that we don't have control, but God does — and He is never late.

Therapeutic Insight

In therapy, we often work with clients on building tolerance to waiting and uncertainty (Linehan, 1993). Our instinct is to move away from discomfort, yet choosing to stay present in the waiting is an act of quiet courage.

Mindfulness during these in-between moments — focusing on the present, breathing deeply, and embracing each opportunity to *be brave* — helps us develop resilience and patience. We begin to see that waiting doesn't mean nothing is happening; it means something deeper is being formed within us.

God uses seasons of waiting to strengthen and steady us. In those spaces where we long for movement, He is doing His best work. Instead of rushing through the discomfort, we learn to face it with courage, trusting that this season of waiting is leading us toward something good.

Reflection Questions

How is God teaching you courage while you are in a season of waiting?

How can you strengthen your ability to patiently trust in God's timing?

What step can you take today to embrace the waiting with courage and hope?

Actionable Step

Choose one small but meaningful act of courage today — something you've been avoiding because it feels uncomfortable: having that difficult conversation, setting a healthy boundary, scheduling that appointment.

Before you take the step, steady yourself with this bold reminder from Joshua 1:9-- Be strong and courageous. Do not be afraid… for the Lord your God will be with you wherever you go.

Let that Scripture be your grounding as you move forward.

Prayer

Lord, waiting can be so difficult, but I choose to trust You in this season. Help me to be strong and courageous as I wait for Your perfect timing. I know that You are renewing my strength, even when I don't see it. Teach me to embrace the waiting, trusting that You are working in me and preparing something good. Give me courage to wait well and hope in Your promises. Amen.

Day 15: Faith Over Feelings

Scripture: "For we live by faith, not by sight." — 2 Corinthians 5:7

"Trust in the Lord with all your heart and lean not on your own understanding; in all your ways submit to him, and he will make your paths straight." — Proverbs 3:5-6

"Do not conform to the pattern of this world, but be transformed by the renewing of your mind. Then you will be able to test and approve what God's will is—his good, pleasing and perfect will." — Romans 12:2

Devotional Reflection

When we first set out on the road, there were many days when I didn't feel like it was the right choice. My emotions were all over the place — fear, doubt, anxiety — and at times, I questioned if we were on the right path. But through it all, God kept reminding me that faith is not about what we feel in the moment. It's about choosing to trust in His promises, even when our feelings tell us something different.

2 Corinthians 5:7 reminds us that we live by *faith*, not by sight (or feeling). Faith isn't about seeing the full picture or feeling a certain way. Our feelings, after all, are based on what we see.

Our feelings can cloud our judgment and lead us to jump to conclusions, often not great ones. But when we place our trust in God's truth, we can move forward with confidence, regardless of *how we feel*. Faith is about trusting God's

Word and His character, even when our emotions try to convince us otherwise.

Therapeutic Insight

In therapy, we use the Cognitive Triangle to help individuals understand how their thoughts, emotions, and behaviors influence one another (Beck, 1976; Burns, 1999).

Each part of the triangle affects the other. So, if we change our behavior, our thoughts and feelings follow. If we change our thinking, our feelings and behaviors follow.

By applying God's Word to our lives, we are changing our thinking, which in turn changes our feelings and behaviors. This is what it means to be transformed by the renewing of your mind.

The Cognitive Triangle, like many other therapeutic concepts, is grounded in biblical truth: When minds are change, everything else changes with it. The bonus for believers is we have the Holy Spirit to lead, guide, remind, and empower us through the renewing and sanctification process.

Reflection Questions

How have your feelings influenced your decisions recently?

In what areas can you choose the renewing of your mind over feelings today?

What promises from God's Word can you hold onto, even when your emotions are uncertain?

Actionable Step

Identify one recurring thought that has been shaping your emotions or behavior lately. Write it down, then find one Scripture that speaks truth into that thought. Say the verse out loud. Choose to allow the Holy Spirit to renew your mind with God's Truth.

Prayer

Lord, I know that my feelings can be all over the place, but I choose today to trust in Your Word. Help me to live by faith, not by sight or feelings. When doubt or fear arises, remind me of Your promises, and give me the strength to stand firm. I trust that You are with me, guiding me through every step. Help me to choose faith, even when my emotions try to lead me astray. Amen.

Melinda Haynes

Day 16: The Gift of Grace

Scripture: "For the grace of God has appeared that offers salvation to all people." — Titus 2:11

"And God is able to bless you abundantly, so that in all things at all times, having all that you need, you will abound in every good work." — 2 Corinthians 9:8

Devotional Reflection

One of the most profound lessons I learned during vanlife was about grace. Grace is one of those things we often talk about in Christian circles, but it's only when we are at our lowest — when we're weak, worn, or feel like we've failed — that we truly experience the depth of its meaning.

There were moments when I when my strength was depleted, when I failed at being a good Christian, and when I questioned every decision I had ever made. But God's grace met me right in the midst of my suffering. He reminded me that His power is made perfect in weakness (2 Corinthians 12:9).

It wasn't about how strong I was or how capable I felt; it was about depending on His strength, His goodness, and His grace. Grace is more than just unmerited favor — it's unmerited favor *by the God who created the Universe*. Think about that for a minute: the one true God, the God that created all things, shows us favor we could never deserve.

No matter what we're going through, God's grace is enough. He is the reason we can keep going when we feel like giving up. He is the reason we can stand, even in the hardest moments.

Therapeutic Insight

In therapy compassion, including self-compassion, is an important concept — it's about recognizing our imperfections, acknowledging our struggles, and offering ourselves the same grace that we would extend to a friend (Neff, 2011).

Just as God extends to us kindness we didn't earn, we can extend kindness to ourselves in moments of weakness or failure. Self-compassion is *not* self-worship, selfishness, or an excuse for bad behavior.

It's a belief that involves accepting that we are not perfect – which is exactly why we need a Savior. And we know that God's love and grace are not based on our performance. Remembering this allows us to stop trying to be "good enough" for Him (as if we ever could be), and to move away from the self-condemnation that keeps us stuck.

Reflection Questions

What is the difference between people who know they have experienced grace and those who don't know that they have?

Where in your life do you need to receive God's grace more fully?

What would it look like if you fully relied on God's grace rather than your own strength in this season?

Melinda Haynes

Actionable Step

Reflect on a time when God offered you grace. If you can't think of a time, ask God to bring a time to your memory. Write the story in your journal along with your feelings of what it is like to receive grace.

Prayer

Lord, thank You for the sufficiency of Your grace. When I feel weak or inadequate, help me to remember that Your grace is all I need. I choose to rely on Your strength today. Help me extend grace to myself and others, just as You have extended grace to me. Amen.

Day 17: When Numbing Out Feels Safe

Scripture: "My flesh and my heart may fail, but God is the strength of my heart and my portion forever." — Psalm 73:26

Devotional Reflection

When we've been hurt deeply, our heart can fail us. We often learn not to feel. Not to want. Not to hope. At some point, shutting down becomes easier than being disappointed again.

Emotional numbness isn't inconsiderate or coldhearted. It is protective. It develops slowly over time—layer by layer, moment by moment—whenever the heart concludes, *"Feeling is unsafe."* And so we disconnect. We move through our routines on autopilot. We stay busy. We distract ourselves. We avoid the discomfort of being fully present in our own lives.

Numbing out can look different for each of us: isolating from people who love us, losing hours to scrolling, binge-watching shows we don't even enjoy, or spending nights absorbed in video games—anything that helps us avoid what hurts, even for a moment. These are temporary shelters, not permanent solutions. They soothe but cannot heal.

Yet Psalm 73:26 invites us back to truth. Even when our flesh and heart fail, God never does. He is the One who restores a weary heart. He is the One who gently awakens what has gone numb. And He is the One who becomes our true Source of comfort—not distraction, not avoidance, but real comfort that reaches the depths of our soul.

God does not shame you for numbing out. He understands why you learned to protect yourself. But He also invites you into something better: safety, presence, and the slow return of feeling anchored in His love.

Therapeutic Insight

In trauma work, emotional numbness is recognized as a "protective shutdown"—a survival response the nervous system uses when pain feels overwhelming or inescapable (van der Kolk, 2014; Fisher, 2017). You are not broken for feeling this way; you adapted. Numbness is not the absence of emotion. It is the mind's attempt to keep you safe when emotions once felt too big to manage.

Healing begins when we create enough safety—both spiritually and emotionally—to feel again, little by little. Grounding practices, supportive relationships, and gentle self-awareness help reopen the pathways that have been shut down.

Spiritually, this mirrors God's invitation to trust Him again… safely, and without pressure. As your nervous system learns safety, your heart becomes free to reconnect with life, hope, and God's comfort.

Reflection Questions

Where do you notice numbness showing up in your life?

What emotions might be hiding beneath your numbness?

How is God inviting you to trust Him again in the places where your heart has grown weary?

Actionable Step

Choose one numbing behavior you often turn to—scrolling, isolating, video games, or something else. Today, pause before you reach for it. Take one deep breath and pray, "Lord, be my comfort right now." Then choose a healthier activity instead (a short walk, stepping outside for fresh air, slow breathing, or praying Psalm 73:26).

Prayer

Lord, You see the places where my heart has grown numb from hurt, exhaustion, and disappointment. Strengthen my heart today. Be my comfort when I'm tempted to shut down. Gently awaken what has gone quiet inside me, and lead me back into trust, hope, and connection with You. Amen.

Day 18: A Life of Purpose

Scripture: "For we are God's handiwork, created in Christ Jesus to do good works, which God prepared in advance for us to do." — Ephesians 2:10

"Many are the plans in a person's heart, but it is the Lord's purpose that prevails." — Proverbs 19:21

"But who are you, a human being, to talk back to God? Shall what is formed say to the one who formed it, 'Why did you make me like this?'" —Romans 9:20

Devotional Reflection

One of the most profound realizations I had during our van travels was that God has a purpose for each step of our lives, even when we can't fully see it. It's easy to get distracted by the chaos of life and wonder if we're on the right path. But the truth is, God's plan for us is always unfolding — sometimes in ways we least expect.

Ephesians 2:10 reminds us that God created intentionally with a divine purpose in mind. He designed us to do good works — specific works that He has already prepared for us to carry out.

Whether those works seem small or monumental, they are all part of His grand design for our lives and His purposes. Living a life of God's purpose doesn't always mean everything makes sense or goes according to our plan.

In fact, sometimes walking in God's purpose means facing pain, confusion, or hardship. There are moments when we don't understand why things are happening, or how the difficult seasons fit into the greater picture. But even in those times, we can trust that God is at work, using every part of our journey to mold us and fulfill His purposes.

Jesus came to give us life to the full (John 10:10), but that doesn't mean it's always easy or without struggle. In fact, our Savior told us that we *will* have trouble in this world (John 16:33). The fullness of life and peace of the Spirit often come through walking by faith, even when, *especially when*, the road is rough or the destination is unclear.

Our purpose is often revealed through the mountains and valleys, as God shapes us into who He wants us to be.

Therapeutic Insight

In therapy, a central theme is finding purpose through pain. Many people face moments of profound difficulty where the road ahead feels uncertain, and the purpose behind their struggles seems unclear. But healing often begins when we embrace the process of growth and trust that, even in hardship, there is purpose.

Sometimes, we can't see the full picture, but purpose is often revealed as we move forward, trusting that God is with us in every step, every tear, and every challenge (Frankl, 1946).

Purpose doesn't always appear when things are difficult, but when we persevere through the hard times, we can remind ourselves that God's ways our higher than our ways (Isaiah 55:8-9) and He has a purpose much bigger than ourselves (Romans 11:33).

Reflection Questions

How can you continue to pursue God's purpose even when it's painful or difficult?

What areas of your life do you find hard to trust God with, and how can you surrender those to Him?

How do you feel God is asking you to trust Him in a new way today?

Actionable Step

Identify one change or challenge in your life that you're resisting. Write a prayer of surrender for that specific area, inviting God into the process. Ask Him for the faith to surrender and persevere.

Prayer

Lord, thank You for the purpose You've woven into my life. I may not always understand the journey, especially when it's hard, but I trust that Your plan for me is good. Help me to live out my purpose even in the difficult moments, knowing that You are with me and that Your good plans will prevail.

Give me the strength to trust You in the pain, and the courage to keep moving forward, even when I don't understand. Thank You for giving me life to the full through Jesus. Amen.

Day 19: Trusting God in Transformation

Scripture: "Therefore, if anyone is in Christ, the new creation has come: The old has gone, the new is here!" — 2 Corinthians 5:17

"Jesus Christ is the same yesterday and today and forever." — Hebrews 13:8

Devotional Reflection

Life is full of transformations — some subtle, others profound. Whether you're experiencing a shift in your career, your relationships, or the way you view yourself or the world, transformation can stir up feelings of uncertainty, fear, and vulnerability.

But one truth remains unwavering: God's presence and faithfulness. 2 Corinthians 5:17 reminds us that in Christ, we are a new creation. The old has gone, and the new has come. This powerful transformation happens when we accept Jesus as our Savior — we are made new from the inside out.

Transformation signifies a deep, spiritual renewal. God is in the business of making all things new, and that includes you. But transformation can also bring discomfort. It's not always easy to embrace the new when the old is familiar, even if it was unhealthy.

Walking in that newness requires us to trust that God is doing a good work in us, even when we don't fully understand the process. Embracing God's unchanging nature allows us to trust that He is faithful to complete the work He started in us.

In a world where everything changes, it's reassuring to know that God never does. Hebrews 13:8 reminds us that Jesus is the same yesterday, today, and forever. While the circumstances of our lives may evolve prompting change in us, His character and love remain constant. During times of transformation, we can rest in His unchanging nature, trusting that He will lead us, guide us, and provide what we need as we walk through the process.

Therapeutic Insight

In trauma-informed therapy, especially approaches like IFS, the heart of healing is inner transformation (Schwartz & Sweezy, 2020). Not transformation for the sake of becoming someone new, but to finally live as the person you were always meant to be.

Transformation matters because the patterns we formed in pain can't carry us into the life God created us for. The defenses that once protected us eventually become the very things that keep us stuck. Healing invites us to release old burdens so we can respond to life from clarity, calm, and truth instead of fear, shame, or survival.

Transformation is the shift from reacting to living.
From self-protection to presence.
From fragmentation to wholeness.
From old wounds directing our story to God leading our steps.

Just as we trust God's unchanging love, we can trust that the transformation, though often uncomfortable, is part of a greater plan.

Reflection Questions

What transformation are you currently experiencing in your life, and how can you trust God in the midst of it?

How can you ground yourself in God's unchanging character when everything feels in flux?

Are there areas in your life where you've been relying on your own understanding instead of trusting God's leading?

Actionable Step

Pick one small action today that reflects trust in God's transforming work—*even if you don't feel ready.* This could be sending the message you've been avoiding, resting when you'd normally push through, saying "no" where you'd usually say "yes," or taking a step toward something healthy that scares you.

Before you do it, pause and pray: "God, I am choosing this step because I trust You to lead me through the transformation."

Prayer

Lord, transformation can feel daunting, especially when I don't understand the changes happening in my life. Help me to trust You completely, knowing that You are with me through every season of growth and change.

Thank You for making me a new creation in Christ. Guide me through this transformation, and help me to trust that You are working all things together for my good. Give me

Melinda Haynes

the peace to rest in Your wisdom and the courage to walk boldly through this season of change. Amen.

Day 20: God's Provision in the Wilderness

Scripture: "See, I am doing a new thing! Now it springs up; do you not perceive it? I am making a way in the wilderness and streams in the wasteland." — Isaiah 43:19

"For I know the plans I have for you, declares the Lord, plans for welfare and not for evil, to give you a future and a hope."— Jeremiah 29:11

Devotional Reflection

Wilderness seasons can be daunting. It's easy to feel lost or abandoned when everything around you seems dry, barren, and unfamiliar. But God, in His infinite wisdom and grace, often chooses to work in wilderness places in powerful ways. When Isaiah declared, "See, I am doing a new thing… I am making a way in the wilderness and streams in the wasteland," he was speaking a prophecy that unfolded in layers.

There was an immediate fulfillment for Israel: God would one day deliver His people from Babylon, lead them through literal deserts, and bring them safely back to their homeland. The "way in the wilderness" and "streams in the wasteland" were not only poetic words—they were promises of real provision for a real journey. Then, in the fullness of time, those same words pointed to Jesus, the Messiah, the ultimate Way-Maker and Living Water. And even now, that same promise continues to reveal God's faithful character toward His people.

This is the richness of God's Word. He speaks into the moment, He speaks toward the future, and He speaks into our personal lives right now. Just because we can't see the way forward doesn't mean God isn't already clearing the path. Wilderness seasons are often the very places where God proves His faithfulness. The same God who delivered Israel from exile and who sent Christ to rescue us from sin is the God who walks with us through our present wastelands.

He brings streams into barren places—not only around us, but within us. Sometimes the new thing God is doing isn't a change in our circumstances but a transformation of our hearts. He refines, restores, and renews us in ways we may not perceive right away.

Jeremiah 29:11 reassures us that God's intentions toward us are good—always. His provision doesn't end when the landscape of our life feels desolate. His presence doesn't withdraw when we feel empty. The same God who carried His people through exile and who brings new life into dry places is walking with you right now.

Therapeutic Insight

In therapy, wilderness seasons often represent times of profound personal growth, where individuals feel disconnected, lost, or stuck. These moments, though difficult, can lead to renewal and self-discovery (Cloud & Townsend, 1992).

Much like how God speaks of bringing streams to the desert, wilderness seasons can allow individuals rediscover strength and resilience, allowing them to perceive growth and new possibilities. It's important to acknowledge that even in the hardest seasons, something new is often springing up — new understanding, new perspectives, and new capacity for healing. Being aware of the potential for growth in the midst of hardship can be empowering.

Reflection Questions

In what ways do you feel you are in a "wilderness" season?

How can you trust that God is doing a new thing in that place, even if you don't see it yet?

How can you shift your perspective to look for the "streams in the wasteland" — God's provision of His Holy Spirit — in your current circumstances?

Actionable Step

Write a prayer of thanks to God, acknowledging the strength and courage He has given you for this wilderness journey. Thank Him for sustaining you, guiding you, and preparing you for the new thing He is doing—even if you cannot see it yet. Let your words reflect trust in His faithfulness: "Lord, thank You for walking with me, strengthening me, and making a way where there seems to be none."

Prayer

Lord, thank You for Your promise that You are doing a new thing, even in the wilderness. And thank You most of all for the best Stream in the wasteland, our Savior, Jesus Christ.

Open my eyes to the ways You are providing and working in my life, even when I can't yet see the full picture, help me to trust You. I lean on Your provision and faithfulness as I walk through this season. Thank You for being my Good Father. Amen.

Day 21: Lay Down Your Weapons

Scripture: " The LORD will fight for you; you need only to be still." — Exodus 14:14

Devotional Reflection

There is a biblical way to guard your heart (Proverbs 4:23), and then there is the survival-driven way many of us learned in seasons of hurt. When caregivers or relationships felt unpredictable or unsafe, we didn't just guard our hearts—we armed ourselves. Not with swords or shields, but with sarcasm, harsh joking, shutting down, taking everything personally, assuming the worst about others, or demanding control so we wouldn't be blindsided again.

These were never "bad" responses—they were protective. They were the only strategies our nervous systems knew. But over time, these weapons begin to harm us more than they help us. They keep people at a distance. They reinforce the belief that we are alone. And they exhaust us emotionally and spiritually.

When God invites us to lay down our weapons, He is not asking us to become unprotected. He is asking us to stop fighting with tools that no longer serve us.

Standing between the Red Sea and Pharaoh's army, the Israelites had no strategy left. Thankfully they didn't need one. All God asked of them was trust: "The Lord will fight for you; you need only to be still."

This kind of stillness isn't passivity—it's surrender. It's choosing to stop reading malice into someone's words when it's really fear talking inside of you. It's choosing not to jump to conclusions about people's motives. It's choosing not to push others away with harsh joking or defensiveness the moment connection feels uncomfortable.

Laying down your weapons is choosing a different way.

You can guard your heart without turning it into a fortress.
You can be wise without being suspicious.
You can be discerning without being defensive.
You can be strong without pretending you don't need anyone.

God does not leave you exposed when you soften. He becomes your defender, your advocate, your protector, your peace. Where you once fought to stay safe, now you can let Him fight for you.

And with every weapon you release, His light protects you.
With every defensive habit surrendered, His love steadies you.
With every moment of trust, He leads you farther into freedom.

He will fight for you.

Therapeutic Insight

In trauma therapy, many of the reactions we label as "problems" are understood as *protective parts*—responses that once helped us survive emotionally overwhelming moments (Schwartz & Sweezy, 2020).

These protectors aren't defective but they are overworked. Their job was to keep you safe when safety was uncertain. But as Bessel van der Kolk (2014) explains, the nervous system often continues reacting to old threats even after the danger has passed. This means your body may still brace for hurt in moments that are actually safe.

Healing begins with compassionate awareness: noticing when a protective response shows up and gently asking, "What is this part of me trying to protect?" As emotional safety grows—through God's presence, healthy relationships, and therapeutic work—these parts no longer have to stay on high alert. They can soften, release old burdens, and make room for healthier patterns of connection.

Laying down your weapons is not losing protection; it is learning that you don't have to live in battle mode anymore.

Reflection Questions

What "weapons" do you want to lay down?

What hurting parts of you are being protected by your weapons?

What would it be like to surrender your weapons to God?

Actionable Step

Choose one protective response you often rely on—harsh joking, withdrawing, or assuming the worst —and pause the next time you feel it rising. Instead of acting on it, take a slow breath and pray quietly: "Lord, help me respond from peace, not protection."

Prayer

Lord, You know the parts of me that have learned to stay armed and ready. Today, I ask for Your help in laying down the weapons that keep me guarded and distant. Teach me how to trust Your protection more than my defenses. Give me wisdom to guard my heart in healthy ways, and courage to release the patterns that aren't aligned with Your Word.

Meet me in the moments I feel tempted to react and remind me that I don't have to fight for myself the way I once thought I had to. Thank You for being my defender, my shield, and my peace. Lead me into a new way of living—one marked by trust, gentleness, and the freedom only You can give. Amen.

Melinda Haynes

Day 22: Trusting God's Sovereignty in Our Circumstances

Scripture: "And we know that in all things God works for the good of those who love him, who have been called according to his purpose." — Romans 8:28

"He has made everything beautiful in its time. He has also set eternity in the human heart; yet no one can fathom what God has done from beginning to end." —Ecclesiastes 3:11

Devotional Reflection

Life is unpredictable. We face unexpected challenges, difficult decisions, and seasons of pain that feel senseless at the time. Yet Romans 8:28 assures us that in all things—both the joyful and the heartbreaking—God is working for our good. This doesn't mean everything that happens *is* good, but it does mean that God, in His sovereignty, can weave purpose out of every thread of our story.

This truth shifts how we see our trials. They are not random or wasted; they become places of growth, refinement, and deeper dependence on God. Embracing this perspective brings peace in the midst of uncertainty.

Sometimes God works things out *around* us, changing circumstances.
Sometimes He works things out *in* us, shaping our character.
And sometimes He works things out *through* others, aligning hearts, timing, and relationships according to His perfect and pleasing will.

No matter the form His work takes, we are never alone. God is with us in every struggle, guiding, strengthening, and using each circumstance to fulfill His purpose in our lives.

Therapeutic Insight

In times of hardship, it's natural to feel overwhelmed or confused by the circumstances we face. Reality Therapy (Glasser, 2000) offers a helpful perspective: while we cannot control what happens to us, we can choose how we respond. This approach emphasizes personal agency, purposeful decision-making, and identifying which choices lead us closer to the life and relationships we genuinely desire.

From a therapeutic standpoint, Reality Therapy invites individuals to look at their current situation and ask, "What is within my control?" and "What choices will move me toward something healthier and more meaningful?" This mirrors the spiritual practice of trusting that God is at work even when we cannot see the full picture. Instead of being consumed by frustration or fear, we learn to focus on the choices we *can* make, aligning our actions with peace, hope, and purpose.

Just as Reality Therapy encourages us to evaluate whether our behaviors bring us closer to our goals, faith invites us to trust that God is shaping something good even in uncertain circumstances. This perspective can create emotional stability in the midst of uncertainty, helping us move forward with clarity, intentionality, and spiritual maturity.

Reflection Questions

In what ways might God be inviting me to respond differently—more intentionally, more calmly, or more aligned with His purpose for me?

Reflect on a recent unpleasant challenge you faced. How might God have used that situation for your good?

How can you shift your perspective to see God's hand at work in your current circumstances?

Actionable Step

Take one challenge you are currently facing and write down how you would see it differently *if you fully trusted* that God is working for your good in this situation. Then speak a simple prayer of alignment: "Lord, help me see this through Your goodness, not my fear." Let this reframed perspective guide one choice or attitude shift you make today.

Prayer

Lord, thank You for Your promise that You work all things together for the good of those who love You and are called according to your purpose. Help me to trust in Your sovereignty, especially when I don't understand my circumstances. Help me let go of my need to understand the bigger picture behind everything in my life. Open my eyes to see Your hand at work in every situation and give me the faith to rest in Your perfect plan. Amen.

Day 23: Joy in Suffering

Scripture: "Consider it pure joy, my brothers and sisters, whenever you face trials of many kinds, because you know that the testing of your faith produces perseverance." — James 1:2-3

"Though He slay me, yet will I trust in Him." — Job 13:15

Devotional Reflection

Experiencing suffering is an inevitable part of the human condition. And God's Word presents us with an exhortation to find joy in it. This call for joy doesn't diminish the reality of pain but rather invites the believer to rejoice in the greatest gift of all: God Himself.

Job's story exemplifies the beautiful experience of deeply knowing God and trusting Him in the worst of earthly circumstances. Despite losing his wealth, health, and family, Job declared, "Though He slay me, yet will I trust in Him" (Job 13:15). His unwavering faith amidst intense suffering highlights that joy isn't the absence of unpleasant circumstances but the presence of complete trust in God's sovereignty.

Similarly, Hebrews 11, often referred to as the "faith chapter," recounts the stories of individuals who endured trials and suffering yet remained faithful. Their lives testify that true joy comes from a steadfast faith that looks beyond present circumstances to the eternal promises of God.

Embracing joy in suffering involves a shift in perspective—recognizing that trials are opportunities for spiritual growth and deeper intimacy with God. It's about choosing to trust in His goodness and purpose, even when the pain is so very real.

Therapeutic Insight

Psychologically, the concept of resilience plays a crucial role in how we navigate suffering. Southwick and Charney (2018) highlight that resilience isn't about avoiding pain, but rather about finding ways to endure, grow, and even thrive through adversity. This aligns with the biblical call to "consider it pure joy" (James 1:2-3), as it emphasizes that suffering can serve as a catalyst for personal growth and spiritual depth.

When we face trials, our brain and body respond to stress, but resilience—developed through faith and perseverance—helps us shift our perspective and find meaning even in hardship.

Job's unwavering faith in the face of his trials is a powerful illustration of God-given resilience. Instead of being consumed by bitterness or despair, Job chose to trust in God's ultimate purpose, demonstrating that joy comes not from escaping suffering, but from cultivating trust and perseverance in the midst of it.

Therapeutically, building resilience involves learning to reframe challenges, seeing them not as threats, but as opportunities to develop inner strength and faith.

Reflection Questions

Reflect on a time when you experienced suffering. How did your faith influence your response?

In what areas of your life is God inviting you to trust Him more deeply?

How can you cultivate a mindset that finds joy in the midst of trials?

Actionable Step

Choose one challenge you're currently facing and write down the situation as it feels right now, then rewrite it from the perspective of joy in the midst of difficulty. See if you can identify at least one possible strength, opportunity, or area of growth God may be developing in you. Reread the joy-filled version every day for one week. Commit also to a daily prayer of surrender: "God, I choose the joy that's only found in You."

Prayer

Lord, I acknowledge the pain and challenges I face, yet I choose to trust in Your sovereignty. Help me to find joy not in the absence of suffering but in the assurance of Your presence and purpose. Strengthen my faith, that I may endure trials with perseverance, hope, and joy. Amen.

Day 24: Waiting Patiently on God's Timing

Scripture: "He has made everything beautiful in its time." — Ecclesiastes 3:11

"When the time is right, I, the Lord, will make it happen." — Isaiah 60:22

"Wait for the Lord; be strong and take heart and wait for the Lord." — Psalm 27:14

Devotional Reflection

Waiting is often one of the most challenging aspects of the Christian journey. In a world that values instant gratification, the call to wait patiently on God's timing can feel countercultural and difficult. Yet, the Scriptures remind us that God's timing is perfect and purposeful.

God's plans are not bound by our schedules. He acts according to His perfect timing, which is always aligned with His wisdom and love. The call to wait isn't passive; it's an active choice to trust in God's sovereignty and goodness. During times of waiting, we are invited to strengthen our hearts, deepen our faith, and rely on God's strength to persevere.

Therapeutic Insight

In the field of psychology, *delayed gratification* is a key concept in emotional and mental well-being. Cozolino (2010) explains that the ability to wait for something we desire—without succumbing to impulsive urges—is crucial for developing emotional regulation, resilience, and long-term satisfaction. This is similar to the spiritual principle of waiting on God's timing and the spiritual gift of longsuffering.

When we actively trust God's sovereignty, our hearts align with His wisdom, which strengthens our patience and deepens our faith. Cozolino's work on brain development highlights that our ability to wait and trust, especially when it's difficult, shapes our emotional maturity and resilience.

In therapy, we help clients build their capacity for delayed gratification, learning to tolerate discomfort in the present for a future reward. Spiritually, waiting on God's timing works similarly, allowing us to develop the patience needed to experience the fullness of His promises in due time.

Reflection Questions

In what areas of your life are you struggling to wait on God's timing?

How can you actively trust and obey God during times of waiting?

What steps can you take to cultivate patience and faith in God's perfect timing?

Actionable Step

Write a brief letter to yourself in the style of Paul's first letter to the Thessalonians. Use his tone of reassurance, steadiness, and encouragement as you remind yourself that:

- What I'm waiting for now is temporary.
- God's timeline is eternal.

- His purposes outlast this moment.

Then check in with yourself: *How is that waiting prayer jar doing?* Add a new slip of paper if needed, noting what you're waiting on God for as you keep your focus on eternity.

Prayer

Lord, waiting is difficult, but I choose to trust in Your perfect timing. Help me to remain faithful and patient as I wait for Your plans to unfold. Strengthen my faith and remind me that You are always at work, even when I can't see it. I trust that in Your time, You will accomplish all that You have promised. Amen.

Day 25: The Power of Forgiveness

Scripture: "Be kind and compassionate to one another, forgiving each other, just as in Christ God forgave you." — Ephesians 4:32

"Bear with each other and forgive one another if any of you has a grievance against someone. Forgive as the Lord forgave you." — Colossians 3:13

"As far as the east is from the west, so far has he removed our transgressions from us."
— Psalm 103:12

Devotional Reflection

Just as burning the ships symbolizes a commitment to a new path, forgiveness is choosing not to drag the past into your future. It means entrusting justice to God instead of holding it in your own hands. Scripture calls us to forgive as we've been forgiven—not as a burden, but as a reflection of the grace we've received.

Forgiveness doesn't ask you to pretend the hurt didn't happen or excuse someone's harmful behavior. It invites you to let go of what's been weighing you down so your heart can rest more fully in God and His goodness.

It's not easy—especially when the wounds run deep. God knows that. That's why He doesn't ask us to forgive alone. We need His strength, and maybe that's the point: *learning to rely on Him in everything.*

Forgiveness is more of a choice than a feeling. And when we choose it, we loosen the chains of resentment and open the door to healing and peace.

Therapeutic Insight

Fred Luskin (2002) explains that forgiveness is primarily a gift we give ourselves. Holding onto grudges or past hurts can cause ongoing emotional pain and stress, preventing us from healing.

Forgiveness involves releasing the grip of resentment, which allows us to move forward emotionally and mentally. Luskin's research shows that by forgiving, we reduce feelings of anger and anxiety, improving both our emotional well-being and physical health.

Choosing forgiveness frees us from the toxic effects of bitterness and opens the door to healing, allowing us to reclaim peace and emotional freedom.

Reflection Questions

Is there someone you need to forgive today?

How can you extend God's grace to others in your life?

What steps can you take to cultivate a forgiving heart?

Actionable Step

Write a letter of forgiveness even if you do not give it to the intended person. You can keep it in your journal or rip it up and throw it away as a symbol of "it is finished."

If you sense God nudging your heart toward further action—sending the letter, initiating a conversation, or extending peace—take time to pray and discern His leading and timing before moving forward.

Prayer

Lord, thank You for the forgiveness You've extended to me through Christ. Help me to forgive others as You have forgiven me. I can't do it alone. I need You! Remove any bitterness from my heart and replace it with compassion and grace. Empower me to live a life that reflects Your love and mercy. Amen.

Day 26: Grieving with Hope

Scripture: "Blessed are those who mourn, for they shall be comforted." — Matthew 5:4

"The Lord is close to the brokenhearted and saves those who are crushed in spirit." — Psalm 34:18

"He heals the brokenhearted and binds up their wounds." — Psalm 147:3

Devotional Reflection

Grief is a natural response to loss, and Scripture never dismisses or diminishes the weight of that pain. Yet the Bible also offers a profound truth: Jesus is not distant from our sorrow—He enters it with us. Jesus Himself declares that those who mourn are blessed because *they will be comforted.* This is not a vague idea or a distant hope; it is a promise given by the One who draws near to the brokenhearted.

In grief, we may feel abandoned or unseen, but Jesus meets us in the very place we feel most shattered. He sits with us in the darkness, holds steady when our world is falling apart, and whispers comfort when words fail us. His presence is not symbolic, it is personal, real, and deeply intimate.

Grief does not push Jesus away—it pulls Him closer. He tends to our wounds gently, patiently, without rushing our process or asking us to just "move on." He makes space for our tears, reminds us we are not alone, and carries us when we have no strength left to take another step.

Though the journey through grief can feel long and heavy, Scripture says we do not grieve as those without hope. Romans 8:18 reminds us that our present sufferings cannot compare with the glory God will reveal. This hope anchors us: not because pain disappears quickly, but because Jesus walks every mile of it with us.

In every tear, every sleepless night, every aching question, *He is near*—closer than breath, steady in love, present in compassion, and faithful to heal what feels impossible to mend.

Therapeutic Insight

According to Worden (2009), grief is a complex, individual process that requires time and emotional work. He explains that healing from grief involves not only feeling the pain but also learning to adjust to life without the loved person, situation, or thing.

This process, while painful, offers the opportunity for growth and transformation. Worden emphasizes that the goal of grieving is not to forget but to find a way to live meaningfully with the loss, integrating it into a new reality.

Grieving with hope means accepting the pain of loss while also looking toward a future of healing. This is supported by research showing that individuals who can hold onto a sense of hope during grief are more likely to experience resilience and find peace.

Grieving is not about rushing to "get over it," but about allowing space for sorrow while nurturing the belief that healing and growth are possible, ultimately leading to renewed joy and purpose.

Reflection Questions

In what ways have you experienced God's presence during times of sorrow?

How can you invite God's comfort into your grieving process?

How can you support others who are grieving, reflecting the comfort you've received?

Actionable Step

List the ways in which you can find joy in the midst of grieving. Write the truth down so you have something to refer to when your feelings lie to you.

Prayer

Heavenly Father, thank You for Your promise to be near to the brokenhearted and to heal our wounds. In our times of grief, help us to feel Your comforting presence and to trust in Your healing power. May we find hope in Your Word and share that hope with others who are mourning. In Jesus' name, Amen.

Day 27: Anger—Harnessing the Power Within

Scripture: "In your anger do not sin: Do not let the sun go down while you are still angry."— Ephesians 4:26

"Whoever is patient has great understanding, but one who is quick-tempered displays folly." — Proverbs 14:29

"Everyone should be quick to listen, slow to speak and slow to become angry." — James 1:19

Devotional Reflection

Anger is a powerful emotion that, when unchecked, can lead to sin, broken relationships, and/or regret. However, the Bible acknowledges anger as a natural feeling and provides guidance on how to handle it righteously.

While anger itself isn't inherently sinful, it's crucial to examine the root causes of our anger. Righteous anger arises from injustice or sin, prompting us to act in accordance with God's will.

Conversely, selfish or uncontrolled anger often leads to harm and should be addressed through repentance and seeking God's guidance.

Jesus exemplified righteous anger when He drove the money changers from the temple, demonstrating zeal for God's holiness. However, He also taught forgiveness and reconciliation, urging us to resolve conflicts and seek peace.

Therapeutic Insight

Lerner (1985) highlights that anger is a natural, healthy emotion that signals a need for change, but it can become destructive if not understood and managed properly. He emphasizes that how we express anger can either build or break relationships.

In his work, Lerner explores the concept of *anger as energy*—an emotion that, when harnessed constructively, can motivate us to address injustices, set boundaries, and take action. The key is learning to process anger before it leads to harmful behavior.

The Bible also teaches us to address anger quickly, not letting it fester (Ephesians 4:26), and to respond with patience and wisdom (James 1:19 and Proverbs 14:29).

Lerner's approach encourages us to pause, reflect, and choose our responses thoughtfully, using anger as a catalyst for positive change rather than a reaction that causes harm.

By managing anger effectively, we transform it from a potentially destructive force into a source of empowerment and growth, enabling us to act in ways that align with our values and bring about healing in relationships.

Reflection Questions

What triggers your anger, and how can you address these triggers constructively?

How can you practice being "quick to listen, slow to speak, and slow to become angry" in your daily interactions?

In what ways can you channel your anger toward righteous actions that align with God's will?

Actionable Step

Make a list of ways you can safely release your anger energy while respecting self and others. Put this list in a place where you will be able to see it often.

Prayer

Lord, grant me the wisdom to recognize and manage my anger in a way that honors You. Help me to respond with patience and understanding, seeking reconciliation and peace. May my emotions serve to draw me closer to You and reflect Your love to others. In Jesus' name, Amen.

Day 28: Living Out Your Faith

Scripture: "In the same way, let your light shine before others, that they may see your good deeds and glorify your Father in heaven." — Matthew 5:16

"Do not merely listen to the word, and so deceive yourselves. Do what it says." — James 1:22

"For we live by faith, not by sight." — 2 Corinthians 5:7

Devotional Reflection

Faith is not just a belief; it's a way of life. As we've journeyed through these devotions thus far, we've explored various aspects of faith—trust, obedience, forgiveness, and more. Now, it's time to put that faith into action.

Living out our faith involves:

> *Serving others:* Look for opportunities to help those in need, whether through acts of kindness, volunteering, or offering support.

> *Speaking truth:* Share the message of God's love and salvation with others, being a witness to His grace.

> *Living with integrity:* Make decisions that honor God, even when no one is watching.

> *Trusting in God's plan:* Even when faced with uncertainty, rely on God's guidance and timing.

Therapeutic Insight

Hayes (2019) in his work on Acceptance and Commitment Therapy (ACT) explains that living in alignment with our values is essential for emotional well-being and personal fulfillment.

According to Hayes, true psychological flexibility comes from acting in accordance with our core beliefs and values, even when faced with difficulties or uncertainty. This aligns closely with the biblical call to live out our faith by not just believing but actively embodying it through our actions.

Hayes emphasizes the importance of commitment to values-based actions—choosing to live in a way that reflects our faith, even when it's hard. This commitment strengthens our emotional resilience and brings a sense of purpose and meaning to our lives.

Faith, when lived out through consistent actions, becomes a powerful force for both personal growth and positive influence in the world.

Reflection Questions

What area of your life is out of alignment with God's Word and are you willing to surrender it today?

How can you actively live out your faith in your daily life?

What are some areas where you can serve others and be a witness to God's love?

Actionable Step

Do one simple act of kindness today — something small, quiet, and intentional. Don't tell anyone else. Let it be between you and God, and let it be a reminder that you choose to live what you believe.

Prayer

Lord, thank You for the gift of faith. Help me to live it out daily through my actions, words, and choices. Empower me to be a light in this world, reflecting Your love and truth. Guide me to serve others and trust in Your plan, knowing that You are always with me. In Jesus' name, Amen.

Day 29: When Efforts Fall Short—Finding Grace in Unmet Expectations

Scripture: "Not by might nor by power, but by My Spirit," says the Lord of hosts. — Zechariah 4:6

"Bear one another's burdens, and so fulfill the law of Christ." — Galatians 6:2

"For I consider that the sufferings of this present time are not worth comparing with the glory that is to be revealed to us." — Romans 8:18

Devotional Reflection

During our van travels, plenty of things went wrong — getting stuck in the sand for hours in Joshua Tree, sliding halfway off a cliff in Utah, a sad deer story in Kansas, a flat tire in Texas, and some wild weather just about everywhere. But one moment stands out. I had planned a fun parasailing day for Katie and my older daughter, Mikayla, who had flown out to meet us in Florida.

While turning "the Beast" around in a crowded parking lot, I was focusing so hard on not hitting anyone — especially the many children running all around — that I completely forgot to look up. A loud crack and metal screech later, I realized I'd driven straight into a low-hanging tree branch.

My instant response was to just lose my cool. But there were plenty of witnesses with cell phones and I didn't want to end up going viral on social media. Jokes aside, I had grown in my faith and in my Christian walk; the Holy Spirit gave me a pause before I responded.

I whispered a prayer, took a deep breath, decided I could deal with the damage and other logistics later... I thanked those who came over to assist, parked the van, and got on that boat. The other adventure guests playfully teased me that I might sink them all with my "bad luck."

I welcomed the good-natured teasing and the laughs that came with it. After all, I was on a *burning* ships journey, not a *sinking* ships one! Besides, I don't believe in luck. I knew that despite the pre-boarding chaos, God was still in control.

The parasailing turned out to be amazingly fun — and thankfully uneventful. No boats were sunk. And, the van repairs were finished within a day.

That day still reminds me how easy it is to forget to "look up" in life, too. We get so caught up in the busyness around us that we miss the simple act of lifting our eyes to God. Yet His grace meets us right there — in the mess, the scrape, the loud crack that reminds us we can't do everything perfectly. And still, He carries us forward.

Despite our best efforts, there are times when things don't go as planned. Guilt, frustration, and inadequacy can hit hard in those moments. But Scripture reminds us that our worth isn't defined by perfect circumstances — it's anchored in God's unwavering love and grace. Our identity is rooted in Christ, not in our successes or failures. When expectations fall apart, His love remains steady, and His grace is always enough.

Therapeutic Insight

Brené Brown (2010) explores the power of vulnerability and self-compassion in her work *The Gifts of Imperfection*. She highlights that embracing our imperfections is essential for emotional well-being. Brown emphasizes that many of us carry feelings of shame and guilt when we fall short of our own or others' expectations. However, true healing comes from letting go of perfectionism and recognizing that our worth is not determined by our successes or failures.

In moments of unmet expectations, it's important to show ourselves the same grace we would extend to others. Brown's research suggests that practicing self-compassion—acknowledging our struggles without judgment—helps us move through disappointment without allowing it to define us.

Like Zechariah 4:6 reminds us, God's strength empowers us even when we fall short, and His grace is the source of our perseverance.

Reflection Questions

What expectations have you placed on yourself that have led to feelings of guilt or inadequacy?

How can you embrace God's grace in areas where you've fallen short?

In what ways can you support others who are experiencing unmet expectations in their own lives?

Actionable Step

What is the next right step you have been putting off due to feeling inadequate or to a past mistake? Can you take that step today?

Melinda Haynes

Prayer

Lord, thank You for Your unwavering love and grace. Help me to release feelings of guilt and disappointment when my efforts fall short. May I find comfort in Your presence and strength in Your forgiveness. Teach me to support others with compassion and grace, reflecting Your love in all circumstances. In Jesus' name, Amen.

Day 30: The Power of Community

Scripture: "And let us consider how to stir up one another to love and good works, not neglecting to meet together, as is the habit of some, but encouraging one another, and all the more as you see the Day drawing near."— Hebrews 10:24-25

"Now you are the body of Christ and individually members of it."— 1 Corinthians 12:27

"How good and pleasant it is when God's people live together in unity!"— Psalm 133:1

Devotional Reflection

Unity fosters a supportive environment where believers can grow, serve, and reflect God's love to the world. Being part of a Christian community provides:

> *Encouragement:* Support during challenging times, uplifting one another in faith.
>
> *Accountability:* Holding each other to biblical standards, helping to grow in holiness.
>
> *Service:* Collaborating to meet the needs of others, both within and outside the church.
>
> *Growth:* Learning together through teaching, discussion, and shared experiences.

Just as a single thread is part of a larger tapestry, each believer contributes to the strength and beauty of the

Church. By engaging in community, we fulfill God's design for His people to live, grow, and serve together.

Therapeutic Insight

In his work, *Siegel (2018)* explores the concept of *interpersonal neurobiology*, emphasizing how our relationships and connections with others are essential for emotional well-being and growth.

He explains that the human brain is wired for connection, and that healthy, supportive relationships help form neural pathways that strengthen emotional resilience, support mental well-being, and foster personal growth.

This is reflected in the biblical call to community, where believers are encouraged to stir one another up in love and good works and to recognize the importance of each individual within the body of Christ.

Siegel's research affirms what believers already know: that the sense of belonging and mutual support found in a community helps individuals feel secure, understood, and empowered. In our *togetherness* spaces, people experience encouragement, accountability, and growth, which are all integral to healing and personal transformation.

Reflection Questions

How has being part of a Christian community strengthened your faith?

In what ways can you contribute to fostering unity and support within your church?

Are there areas where you can encourage or serve others in your community?

Actionable Step

Do something for your community this week. You could donate or volunteer at a shelter, roll the neighbor's trash can up their driveway, join a neighbor for coffee, or post an inspirational quote on your community's social media page.

Prayer

Lord, thank You for the gift of community. Help me to actively engage with fellow believers, offering encouragement, support, love, and healing to others as I continue to heal as well.

May our unity reflect Your love to the world and strengthen our collective faith. Guide me to serve and build up the body of Christ, fulfilling Your purposes. In Jesus' name, Amen.

References

Amabile, T. M., & Kramer, S. J. (2011). *The progress principle: Using small wins to ignite joy, engagement, and creativity at work*. Harvard Business Review Press.

Beck, A. T. (1979). *Cognitive therapy and the emotional disorders*. Penguin Books.

Bowlby, J. (1988). *A secure base: Parent-child attachment and healthy human development*. Basic Books.

Brown, B. (2010). *The gifts of imperfection: Let go of who you think you're supposed to be and embrace who you are*. Hazelden Publishing.

Brown, B. (2012). *Daring greatly: How the courage to be vulnerable transforms the way we live, love, parent, and lead*. Gotham Books.

Burns, D. D. (1999). *The feeling good handbook* (Rev. ed.). Plume.

Carnes, P. (1997). *The betrayal bond: Breaking free of exploitive relationships*. Health Communications, Inc.

Cloud, H., & Townsend, J. (1992). *Boundaries: When to say yes, how to say no to take control of your life*. Zondervan.

Cozolino, L. (2010). *The neuroscience of psychotherapy: Healing the social brain* (2nd ed.). W. W. Norton & Company.

Dana, D. (2021). *Polyvagal exercises for safety and connection: 50 client-centered practices*. W. W. Norton & Company.

Fisher, J. (2017). *Healing the fragmented selves of trauma survivors: Overcoming internal self-alienation*. Routledge.

Frankl, V. E. (2006). *Man's search for meaning* (I. Lasch, Trans.). Beacon Press. (Original work published 1946)

Glasser, W. (2000). *Reality therapy in action*. HarperCollins.

Hayes, S. C. (2019). *A liberated mind: How to pivot toward what matters*. Avery.

Hayes, S. C., Strosahl, K. D., & Wilson, K. G. (2016). *Acceptance and commitment therapy: The process and practice of mindful change* (2nd ed.). Guilford Press.

Kabat-Zinn, J. (1990). *Full catastrophe living: Using the wisdom of your body and mind to face stress, pain, and illness*. Delacorte Press.

Levine, P. A. (2015). *Trauma and memory: Brain and body in a search for the living past*. North Atlantic Books.

Lerner, H. G. (1985). *The dance of anger: A woman's guide to changing the patterns of intimate relationships*. Harper & Row.

Linehan, M. M. (1993). *Skills training manual for treating borderline personality disorder*. Guilford Press.

Luskin, F. (2002). *Forgive for good: A proven prescription for health and happiness*. HarperOne.

Neff, K. D. (2011). *Self-compassion: The proven power of being kind to yourself*. William Morrow.

Neimeyer, R. A. (2001). *Meaning reconstruction and the experience of loss*. American Psychological Association.

Porges, S. W. (2011). *The polyvagal theory: Neurophysiological foundations of emotions, attachment, communication, and self-regulation*. W. W. Norton & Company.

Schwartz, R. C., & Sweezy, M. (2020). *Internal family systems therapy* (2nd ed.). Guilford Press.

Siegel, D. J. (2010). *The whole-brain child: 12 revolutionary strategies to nurture your child's developing mind*. Delacorte Press.

Siegel, D. J. (2012). *The mindful brain: Reflection and attunement in the cultivation of well-being*. W. W. Norton & Company.

Siegel, D. J. (2018). *Aware: The science and practice of presence*. TarcherPerigee.

Southwick, S. M., & Charney, D. S. (2018). *Resilience: The science of mastering life's greatest challenges* (2nd ed.). Cambridge University Press.

Snyder, C. R. (2002). *Hope theory: Rainbows in the mind. Psychological Inquiry, 13*(4), 249–275. https://doi.org/10.1207/S15327965PLI1304_01

van der Kolk, B. (2014). *The body keeps the score: Brain, mind, and body in the healing of trauma*. Viking.

Worden, J. W. (2009). *Grief counseling and grief therapy: A handbook for the mental health practitioner* (4th ed.). Springer Publishing Company.

Appendix – References by Topic

Trauma bonding — Carnes, P. (1997). *The Betrayal Bond: Breaking Free of Exploitive Relationships.*

Glimmers — Dana, D. (2021). *Polyvagal Exercises for Safety and Connection.*

Music and emotional regulation — Levitin, D. J. (2006). *This Is Your Brain on Music.*

Unfinished business & acceptance — Neimeyer, R. A. (2001). *Meaning Reconstruction & the Experience of Loss.*

Survival mode — van der Kolk, B. (2014). *The Body Keeps the Score.*

Naming the wound — Brown, B. (2012). *Daring Greatly.*

Hope as a psychological construct — Snyder, C. R. (2002). *Hope Theory: Rainbows in the Mind.*

Exposure to fear builds resilience — Siegel, D. J. (2010). *The Whole-Brain Child.*

Uncertainty tolerance — Hayes, S. C., Strosahl, K. D., & Wilson, K. G. (2016). *Acceptance and Commitment Therapy (2nd ed.).*

Social support and perceived presence — Bowlby, J. (1988). *A Secure Base: Parent-Child Attachment and Healthy Human Development.*

Small wins & progress — Amabile, T. M., & Kramer, S. J. (2011). *The Progress Principle.*

Mindfulness & pausing — Kabat-Zinn, J. (1990). *Full Catastrophe Living.*

Cognitive reframing — Beck, A. T. (1979). *Cognitive Therapy and the Emotional Disorders.*

Waiting & distress tolerance — Linehan, M. M. (1993). *Skills Training Manual for Treating Borderline Personality Disorder.*

Faith over feelings & CBT — Beck, A. T. (1979). *Cognitive therapy and the emotional disorders.* Penguin Books.

Burns, D. D. (1999). *The Feeling Good Handbook.*

Self-compassion — Neff, K. D. (2011). *Self-Compassion: The Proven Power of Being Kind to Yourself.*

Emotional numbness — Fisher, J. (2017). *Healing the fragmented selves of trauma survivors: Overcoming internal self-alienation.* Routledge.

van der Kolk, B. (2014). *The body keeps the score: Brain, mind, and body in the healing of trauma.* Viking.

Finding purpose through pain — Frankl, V. E. (1946). *Man's Search for Meaning.*

Embracing Transformation — Schwartz, R. C., & Sweezy, M. (2020). *Internal family systems therapy* (2nd ed.). Guilford Press.

Wilderness as personal growth — Cloud, H., & Townsend, J. (1992). *Boundaries.*

Lay Down Your Weapons — Schwartz, R. C., & Sweezy, M. (2020). *Internal family systems therapy* (2nd ed.). Guilford Press.

Van der Kolk, B. A. (2014). *The body keeps the score: Brain, mind, and body in the healing of trauma.* Viking.

God's sovereignty & trust in uncertainty — Glasser, W. (2000). *Reality therapy in action.* HarperCollins.

Joy and resilience in suffering — Southwick, S. M., & Charney, D. S. (2018). *Resilience: The Science of Mastering Life's Greatest Challenges.*

Waiting and nervous system regulation — Cozolino, L. (2010). *The Neuroscience of Psychotherapy.*

Forgiveness and emotional release — Luskin, F. (2002). *Forgive for Good.*

Grieving with hope — Worden, J. W. (2009). *Grief Counseling and Grief Therapy.*

Anger as energy and signal — Lerner, H. G. (1985). *The Dance of Anger.*

Living out values in action — Hayes, S. C. (2019). *A Liberated Mind.*

Grace and unmet expectations — Brown, B. (2010). *The Gifts of Imperfection.*

Power of community and connection — Siegel, D. J. (2018). *Aware: The Science and Practice of Presence.*

About the Author

Melinda Haynes is a seasoned therapist, founder and executive director of Family & Children's Counseling Services, and the author of several transformative books in the Christian self-help genre.

With an MA in Counseling Psychology and professional licensure in three states, Melinda has spent over two decades helping individuals and families heal from trauma and build healthier lives.

www.MelindaHaynes.com

www.ingramcontent.com/pod-product-compliance
Lightning Source LLC
Chambersburg PA
CBHW022121040426
42450CB00006B/793